Another Lens

Noctis Dancer

BookLeaf Publishing

India | USA | UK

Presentation by *BookLeaf Publishing*

Web: www.bookleafpub.com

E-mail: info@bookleafpub.com

ISBN: 9789363311800

First edition 2024

To My Dad.

Part of me still waits for you.

I do not think I will ever stop.

(01/11/20)

ACKNOWLEDGEMENT

I naturally want to acknowledge and thank my family, who is endlessly supportive, my best friend, Chandler, who is always sending me the best art to look at, and my mentor, Doctor Porter, who has allowed me to reach levels of notice I am constantly shocked by. All of whom have supported my writing and other creative projects endlessly!

But most of all, this book would not exist without my (equally) best friend, Maggie.

Maggie assisted me in the research for this poetry book, and her support was vital in not only helping me begin the project by encouraging me to take the writing challenge and trust myself and my poems but also seeing it through to completion and helping me bring it to life.

Maggie is one of those people where, once you finally understand each other, you do not ever know how you existed without them. Maggie is endlessly supportive of me, my art, my creative projects, and oftentimes even inspires them or helps me find new subjects or ideas within them. Maggie is responsible for helping me research the history behind many of the poems in this book, including but not limited to Gilgamesh & Enkidu, David & Jonathan (as well as the companion poems), the history behind Cain, and more. I would not have fully realized this book without it. Thank you, Maggie. If you don't cry reading this I'm going to have to try harder to fully explain the levels at which you are truly incredible.

Additionally, thank you to the reader for taking a chance on this book. I can only hope that you enjoy it! And if you don't, I personally recommend writing scathing hate comments within its pages, I personally find that to still offer a fulfilling experience. Much love either way!

PREFACE

Please note that these poems contain blood & violence and some of them have intentionally unsettling undertones!
This collection of poems is intended as a love note to the original stories and ideas borrowed within, not a critique or demolishing. With that in mind, I hope you enjoy these re-tellings and reimaginings, and find them earnest and adoring.

Medusa

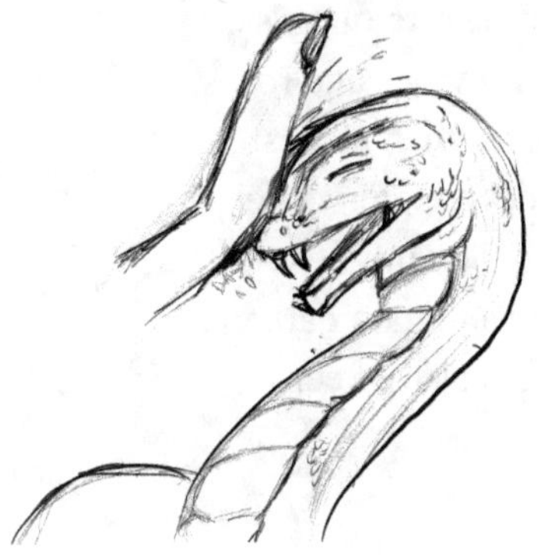

There is a place, far from the heavens, where my
lover now resides
I have never seen her body, though, I have never
really tried
my lover was fragmented by the staining touch
of man
and they call her 'monster' so unbidden,
for they cannot understand

She kisses my worn fingertips,
apologies to broken nails,
and when the coils of her hair touch me,
I feel desperate softness in their tails,
they nuzzle and caress me,
a tongue flicks over my closed eyes,
whispers sweet nothings to the darkness,
to these empty lids of mine.

The stone stillness all around us,
casts a softness to our kiss,
tangled with vines and roses,
better statues than as flesh,
they can never again covet
that which they might see,
and can never again darken
the secrets that we keep

Gilgamesh & Enkidu

Though breath becomes short,
and flesh becomes weak,
I pray, as my heart struggles to beat,
and my blood sings its pain,
that you know now I would give even my life
for the sole gift of having known you

You are the crack of thunder from the
unforgiving sky,
you are the bolt of lightning that ignites dusted
fields,
you are the downpour of tears as the gods fear
you and weep,
you are the breaking of the heavens as your
storm drives out their light

and to me, my love,
you are the warmth of battle-warmed skin,
the taste of blood when we kiss, ravaging yet
intimate,

forceful yet giving,
you are the possessively gentle curl of your arm
at my waist,
soft with sleep,
bitter at my pain,
you are the hand that brushes away my
sweat-soaked hair
as I am wracked with fever,
as I am coming to die.

You look at me in a way I do not think any one
person has ever looked at another before
you look at me like you will not allow me to
succumb,
that if the gods stole me from you
you would break them in hand,
and tear immortality from their flesh,
and place it in my chest beside a heart that has
long belonged to you,
just as I do,
just as yours belongs to me.

I tell you now,
that as long as you live, in that way,
so will I.
That if immortality finds you,
then truly,
I shall never die.

Icarus & Apollo

My father warns me of the sunlight,
of the warmth of his embrace
but with freedom so near,
I ache only for his face,
when my wings fragment with reckoning
and I am punished for my need,
I'm simply bathing in his touch,
satiate my deepest greed

As the sea rises to crush me,
I know only rays of light,
displaced through icy waters,
though bereft of any flight,
His warmth will still consume me
as is his given right
for I'd give every piece to him
his touch my farthest height

So even as my father,
screams my name and curses him,
I hear only Apollo's whisper,
the soft weight of my great sin,
With burning feathers all around,
I know only my love's claim
will never crave another sound
for this death is only skin.

The Sphynx

Each morning the sun rises
and my lover poses her query
the same question I must answer
though I never do grow weary

She asks me for my life
and I sadly must decline
although I'd give her everything
just to call her mine

She aches with every year
as my flesh begins to age
ever easier her questions
as my mind starts to decay

As I answer this one wrong
I do hope she will forgive me
She is my ferry to the end
I simply wanted her here with me

The Four Horsemen

There is war in my blood,
war in my body
born in it, born for it
I'd kill anybody
There is no life that's spared
in the hell we hath wrought
Of the man that I could be
of the man I am not

I am sick these days,
sicker than most
I infect what I touch
and I burn what I don't
and all of these ghosts buzzing freely around me
slick in my lungs and spill wet down my throat

And I have marched for days,
so like a dog, I am hungry,
teeth gnashing with spit
So starved my mouth foaming
with blood and with acid
it melts the world red
And I am craven and wicked,
so I bite off their heads

And then I'm becoming
the poison, the rot
Cheeks gaunt and eyes misty
maybe dead,
maybe not
The sickness consumes
everything that I'm touching
'Til I carve out their hearts
'til I bite and they're nothing

And when the Four Horsemen find me in my
grave
nails blunt and flesh withered
skin ripe with decay
They will gladly applaud me
for the things that I've done
and they will let me burn swiftly
in the light of the sun

Ruth & Naomi (I)

They will not say we are lovers.
They will say we were companions,
they will say we were close.
But if not for you, I'd be fragments of myself.

Intertwined, we are eternal,
Even as l ache to draw you ever closer,
I find truth in your skin,
I find home in your body.

They will not understand us, love,
but I do not let it sting.
I understand us, love,

Through hearts that beat for us both,
through a circuit of endlessness that drives me to
you,
my breaths are your breaths,
my blood is your blood,
my body is your body,

And sin cannot find us here.

If heaven is forbidden to us,
I have no need.
You are my scripture,
your voice my prayer,
And if you find a lover,
he, too, shall be mine.

We three wrapped in symphonic chords
struck by angel's voices,
of church steeples and ringing bells,
statues poised as if in waiting,
wings risen to unblinking stars,
I see you, there.
I hear you, there.

The bell-whisper of your laughs,
the slow choir of our voices.
What is worship, if not this?
If not us?
He, you, I—

Surely the lord would not deny us happiness,
Surely the lord would see the sanctimony of our
union,
and he would smile.

This is not a sin, Ruth.
There is nothing holier than this.

David & Jonathan (II)

We are weapons of war,
swifter than eagles,
stronger than lions,
the hard edge of a blade,
We are not men,
We are tools, you and I,
We are the plagues they release to win the battle,
we are the violence they impart to win the
world.

But in your arms, we are different.
Knit together, we are softened,
though a cutting edge never dulls,
we lie together and we are whole,
we are gentle,
we are sweet.

Our bodies are as one,
two halves of one soldier,
more than love,
more than thought,
we are ephemeral, I know,
and yet I ache to let it linger.

Your clothes still smell of your skin,
Even as they meld to my shape,
and I can tell that Michal knows it,
even as she wraps her arms around me,
guides me to escape,
'Go to him,' she tells me,
and I know it must sting,
and yet I can only think of you.
I see your eyes in hers,
your smile on her lips,
for you are in everything I do.

We make our covenant,
I in your clothes,
shared blood soaking into our veins,
our fingers interlocked, emblazoned with red,
it slinks down my finger,
a ring forged of our melding,
and you look at me as if I am made of stars.
As if I am more than anything you've ever
known.

You whisper eternity into our kiss,
and I breathe infinity onto your lips,
and for a moment, we are endless.
Beyond death,
beyond war,
in you I find peace, ceaselessness.
I know, easily, I will love you in every life-
I am certain I always have.

Michal (III)

As she watches him escape to his lover,
embraced in his clothes,
wrapped in his scent,
she still cannot love any other.

The ghost of him still lies in their bed,
the sheets laden with his imprint,
and beside it, she rests her head,
and wishes she were different.

She wishes she were more,
she wishes she were less,
She'd be anything he wants of her,
she'd do anything he asked.

Even in the gaze of another,
she can only find his eyes,
yet she cannot be his lover,
though desperately she tries

Is this the pain of loving?
the crushing weight to have a heart?
this empty thing she's craving?
this never-ending, never-start?

To have and then to hold,
and yet he'll never dare
in sickness and when old,
and yet he'll never care

The pain of femininity
Cast there upon the street
He finds her words in enmity
as she prostrates at his feet

And yet the cleave of brutal blade
does not free her of her want
she is nothing, yes, his point is made,
she will never be enough

Achilles' Rage

Maybe Achilles' rage, was so
pungent, so impossible to understand
for many years and by many men
because inherently his rage came from his
mother.

Deeper than bone,
More everlasting than existence itself.

Achilles burned with deep, endless hatred for the
rest of his life, many days and nights left lying
beside nothing more than a body,
Achilles sought not to simply destroy, but to
obliterate,
to be so destructive Hector's very bloodline
would feel it,
to be so profoundly cruel that not even the gods
could stomach it,

Achilles' rage was so monumental that the gods
feared him as he dragged Hector's body,
as he tore apart Troy.

Perhaps he learned this from his mother.
From her fear and her hate.

Could it be said that this is how he learned to be
angry?

Achilles had no father that mattered.
No father by blood, at least.
Achilles was his mother,
betrayed and beautiful, perfect and poisonous.
And even if Patroclus forgave Achilles
for the cruelty of letting him die,

Achilles never would.

Leda

How beautiful were you when he first saw you?
Dappled with the kiss of the sun,
filtered through the verdant overcast,
the tangle of leaves overhead,
the endlessness of life.

Do you ache with longing for the moments
before?
The sparse, precious seconds in which you did
not know the cruelty of gods?
How many breaths did you take in the seconds
before he approached?
The final breaths of serenity, the last dying
instances of tranquility?

When you tilted your head toward the trees,
and heard the birds in the branches above,
the magnetic song of silent apology
from an anticipatory sky,
did you know what it would be like to catch
sight of the clouds again?

When you lift your head toward the heavens,
do you hate?
The clouds are stagnant, congealed over your
shaking body,
and you wish to pull the lightning from them
with your bare hands,
to tear away the blue and find the forgiveness of
midnight
to relinquish the betrayal of day into the
anonymity of night

The mourning slivers of moonlight
that cradle your face and stand vigil to your pain
the moon shrouds you in shivers of silver
and yet she lets you cry watchlessly
allows you the privacy of sorrow

You pray to never be beautiful again.

Antonius & Hadrian

I'd write a thousand books for you
Fuss over every little piece
If you desired the moon, my love
I'd even grab it with my teeth

I'd carve epitaphs of your radiance
Sculptures of your shape,
I'd make perfumes of your fragrance,
I'd make masks of your sweet face

You are eternal, caught by artist's hand
You are the muse, eternal light
You are the poem, spoken reverent,
You are the day, you are the night

They will remember, this I swear to you,
For stone does not decay,
And I will carve your face each day anew
To ensure that you will stay.

Sun & Moon

Are you there?
It has been some time since we last met.
I see you, in the distance, glittering, eternal and
so beautiful, yet
You're bound to another's wicked path, to salten
sick regret,
to dark and boundless silence,
for the night is all you get.

With me, you could be happy—golden, glowing,
warm

I'd have you and I'd hold you,
I swear to do no harm,
to always watch your dancing,
every hour, night and day,
I'd never leave you glancing,
unsure if I will stay.

I promise not to close my eyes,
I won't even stop to blink,
to make up for endless lonely nights,
I would not sleep a wink,
and when your stinging ocean tears
flood the earth and dry
it gives those who didn't value you
such a pretty last goodbye.

Siren & Sea

In blessed rapture, I send them to you,
To the depths to hide their screams,
You are the only thing that cradles me,
The only thing I ever need

Men could never understand you
the way you understand me,
They desecrate your perfect shape
I'll let them fill you when they bleed

They try to take from me,
as they take from you,
as I pull them through the deep,
as I'm held by you, your endless blue,
you are the breaths I breathe

I'll protect you with my everything
From those wretches up above,
I'll keep them from divesting you
of your kindness and your love

Hanahaki

I love you so much I'd cough up flowers
I'd let the vines twist around my guts
I'd let their petals spell "I love you"
as they glisten with my blood

You could paint me in the colors
of my aching, bleeding heart,
as I wish you were my lover
and you're happy that you aren't

The red tones all around me,
of flowers and of flesh,
simply make you look so pretty
that I'm happy that I've bled

And love of mine, I say sincerely,
even if you'd never know
I'd choose you over life so quickly
your lack of love would never show

Lucifer & Cain

He was the first
and so was I—
the first to fall from opal sky
the first to taste the flames of hell
the first to hate and do it well

The rough stone in my hands not shaking
he tells me life must be worth taking
And I've never heard of death before
so I want to taste it even more

They love my brother more than me
they cast him into sanctity
If this is the plan that God hath brought

he should not be shocked by the path he's
wrought
for if sinning doth a sinner make
was I born unfavored, born to break?
was satan made to be pushed away?
created just for hell's front gate?

The tang of blood, when known by dogs,
often foretells the end,
and now that I have known it too,
I find I understand.
The rock split skin
and I found blood there
glazed along my teeth
and the stinking rot, it permeates
every breath that I now breathe,

and I'll ask Lucifer, in hell,
why he chose this fate for me
and he'll ask if I found beauty there
in the red that soaked the field
when I kneel in the dust of aftermath
if I regret the choice to steal

and I'll never know what to say to him
as he gently cups my face
as he holds me closer than God ever did
as I find warmth in his embrace

I know something is wrong with me
something distorted by my kill
And I know that I should pull away
as I know I never will
discarded as I was by them,
even satan's touch felt sweet
And though he knows that I regretted it
and flames lick at my feet
He still holds me in his wicked arms
cruelly, I am complete

Jesus & Judas

The grief of you is an ambient force.
more volatile than the wrath of angels,
more damning than the sins of man.
Grief is in the trees, in the air,
it tangles with the sunrise
and it kisses me goodnight

Judas, my grief for you is like breathing,
sometimes I forget it's even there,
so busy I am with the world,
until suddenly, it's catching,
and tinder turns to flame.

What did I do to deserve the loss of you, Judas?
I have returned—life sings in my veins,
pooled in goblets,
and yet when I stepped free of my tomb,
you were gone.

You had become the whisper in the air
after the beat of a bird's wing,
and I beg to catch you,
to grasp the echo of your voice only once more.

I had thought if my father needed a martyr
he would find one in me
but if you, who I crave,
more than life,
more than death,
are not forgiven by my dying
I do not want to be redeemed.

Magdalene

Mary Magdalene is a muse,
She is opalescence and vibrancy
She is the wash of sunlight over the crushing
black sky
and the streak of comets that chase away the fog
strangling and muting the cosmos

She illuminates even the shyest of stars
and pulls them onto a stage of majesty and
melody
that they'd never thought they'd see

She is the glittering crack of fireworks on the
horizon
lighting up the bay in shades of color mankind
has only ever dreamed of
Her luminescence makes the crowd cheer, makes
them sing, they kiss and they dance and they
pray for another year of her beauty and mind

She is the viridescent fields that tangle through
the tiniest fawn's legs as it bounds forth and
nuzzles its mother
She is the doe that lowers her head, urging her
young forward, a softly guiding force, dappled
sunlight on their tawny silken coats

She is the moon spilling silver rays over each
footpath, smiling through her winking crescent,
ensuring passerby don't trip
and even through gossamer strands of overcast
sky,
they all know she is there,
they all feel her presence
hear her voice and feel her warmth even in the
emptiest of rooms or the most solitary of forests

She is the breeze winding through the treetops,
fluffing fresh downy feathers and breathing
softly under outspread wings, carrying the song

of nature like the chiming chorus of windswept
bells

She is the most human of gods, vigilant to
suffering, running gentle fingertips over aching
wounds and mended bones,
the voices of angels poised on her tongue,
holy, chromatic prisms of light streaking across
her shape
casting sun-flares of rainbows over every
waking moment,
even when the darkness smothers the glow

She is there, in the shadow, the warmth of word
and the chords of melody
for she is in everything
for she is color, and light, and sound
because that is simply who she is

My Magdalene,
I am her instrument, her word incites in me the
primal understanding of life
In lengths at which I had never discovered
And I ache with the want to know her
even if not in flesh,
for even astride the messiah, my gaze lingers on
her,
on her quick-whip grin and her sparkling eyes,
and I know she is abundant,

and human,
and living,

and I know that she is in everything,
and I know that she is boundless
and breathing
and I am glad to have lived in the same
heartbeats as she

For there is no better muse than my Magdalene,
she is the poetry that urges my hand
and she is the figure which inspires my sculpture
and she is holy and imperfectly exact in a way
that even the lord cannot be
for she is not born a savior, or god, or angel,
but instead a mortal, like me,
and thus her acts of good are righteous and
resounding
in a way that is Chosen rather than Destined,

And she is the light in all things,
tilting the prism and catching the sun,
purely because that is how she has decided to be.

Bloody Mary

You are disgusting, misshapen and ugly, I say.
You are hideous. I hate you. You have tortured
me for lifetimes, I say.

There is nothing worse than you, I say.
She always says it back.
We say it at the same time.

Our mouths move in sync.
You're psychotic, I say, and angry—you're
always so angry.

You won't stop mimicking me.
I raise my hand to touch you.
The silver glass is freezing, where we touch.
You're cold, I spit, You're so cold.

Beat against the surface.
She will kill you if you don't get to her first.

Tears in her eyes, she beats against the glass
harder and harder,
there's salt in your mouth,
on your face,
in your eyes.
blood of grief,
streaking onto your lips.

Great heaving sobs,
and you shatter the mirror where that other girl
lived.

Was she ever there at all?
Did I spin around three times?
Say her name, watch her manifest?
Will she be in the next mirror I see?

Was she ever there at all?

Shape-Shifter

I know not where it comes from,
I know not what I will find,
As I am rushing through the forest,
after trails it leaves behind,

The oaken limbs will reach for me
as I follow songs of screams,
they will pull and yank with apathy,
they will worm into my dreams,

The beast I find I'm racing
is the most wretched kind of all,
am I running or am I chasing
do I wail or do I call?

It left blood upon my doorstep,
it left skin upon my floor,
And it left behind only corpses,
of the things I'd loved before,

It took my skin, it must've,
for I know not who I am,
things I did I never could have,
things I'd never understand

I lunged forward far too quickly
as he struck out with his fist
a man who said he loved me
a man whose strike had never missed,

and I watched him as he struggled
as he grew silent and then still
Yet these actions left me puzzled
I've never fought and never will

So I hunt these wicked creatures
throughout the days and every night
The one that took my features
Who forced my hand to fight

And though no one else can see it,
and tell me I'm not in the wrong,
I'm sure it could be defeated,
though I have never quite been strong

For I would never kill my lover,
through bruises and through shame
through nights he became crueler
as he cursed my very name

So I look for this shape-changer
for this thing that stole my face
and in the mirror, I am a stranger
through the relief I cannot place

Grim Reaper

There is something at the end of everything,
whether it is darkness,
or heaven,
or reincarnation,

There is surely something there that will know
who I am and what I have done—
there is something that will further me into
cessation,
whether it is chemical, or skeletal, baring a long,
winged scythe,
or poised upon a boat, set to carry me away,

I will look at the grim reaper,
or the ferryman of souls,
or whatever breathes between this world and the
next,

I will look into the darkness of empty,
before my eyes fall shut,
and I will say,

"Did you know?"

And I won't know what I'm asking,
the chemical bursts of sunlight and lunar smile
the thunder-quick flash of all of the pain
and the softness
and the breaking
and the shattered clouds of dying stars

will look back at me
with bleached-pale bones
and icy-warm eyes,
and it will say,

"Yes."

Like it's been asked a thousand times before.
As if rehearsed.
And I will cry,

pools of grief streaking down my bloodless face

and Death will watch me, silently,
as I come apart
as I filter in through the cracks of everything I
was and everything I ever will be,
and the ferryman will say,
"Yes," again, with something bittersweet and
physical, "I knew."

Instead, like it had never even doubted.
and the tears will stop
and the aching will cease

and I will return to the vision of godhood that
had arrested me
from the very moment it had all fallen to pieces
and I will say,

"Okay." As if I've said it a thousand times
before.
As if rehearsed.
As if it was never in doubt.
And the serpent coiled at the base of eternity,
the jackal-headed diviner of endlessness,
the whispered ache of 'too soon' and 'a moment
longer,'
the pomegranate-red lips of fate and destiny,

That which is between this world and the next,
will know all that I have done
and all that I will do
and it will not have been in vain.

"Not yet." It says, firmly.

And as I stare into the misty skies of the empty,
I will know it is with kindness.
"Not yet." I agree.

And when I wake, from a sleep not unlike the
end, I know I will see it again.
But not yet.

Soulmates

My soulmate's name on one wrist
my worst enemy on the other
and both of them are your script
for there will never be another

You are that which will destroy me,
You are the most sane I've ever felt,
You are the ice that consumes my body,
You are the flames in which I melt.

There is disaster inside your body,
and calamity poised on your tongue,
You are the viciousness of understanding
and the wicked hate of love.

You are the ending of my story
and the beginning of the rest
The storm that floods my temple
the sun that dries the nest.

You are the cruelty of knowing
that no one else will be enough
to fill my heart with loathing
kiss me sharp and mean and rough

Your soul mark on each arm,
and your voice within my veins,
And even though you harm
I'd never want another name

The Lovers

I wish I could be loved in the way Patroclus and
Achilles tried to, in the way Antonius and
Hadrian did, in the way the moon loves the sun,
in the way Apollo loved Icarus,
the way hot wax spills over steaming skin

If I cannot be your one and only
Can I be the villain to your heroic protagonist?

I'd do it, if you let me—
unleash evil so you could vanquish it,
become darkness so your light could overcome
it,
watch you from afar as you gained the strength
to beat me
and when our swords clashed and sparks lit up
your snarling face,

god, I would want to kiss you

taste the tang of my blood
in the shape of your lips
and in that, you'd be mine
as the blade falling over my neck,
you'd be mine.
I'd pray that my blood on the ancient stones of
our battleground
caused you to slip
just so I could hold you
feel the flesh so carefully formed
perfect to cleave my head off with

I want to be that for you
I want to be the worst thing you've ever known
and the most heroic thing you've ever done
and I want to love you for it.